Supernatural Scotland: Shakespeare's Macbeth

First Witch

Second Witch

Third Witch

Macbeth

Banquo

Ross

Angus

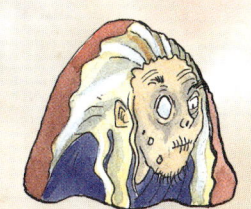

Hecate

First Apparition

Second Apparition

Third Apparition

Introducing the story of Macbeth ...

At the start of the play, Macbeth is a brave soldier who has just been fighting a battle in support of King Duncan of Scotland.

The story ...

The three witches plan to meet Macbeth after the battle. We find out that they have supernatural powers and are ruled by other spirits.

What might the characters be thinking ...?

"When shall we meet? What shall we do? How can we cause trouble for Macbeth?"

Useful words ...

hurlyburly confusion

ere before

heath a common, or open land

Graymalkin traditional name for a witch's cat

Paddock name for a witch's familiar, probably a toad

anon I'm coming now

Macbeth Act 1, Scene 1

An open place.

Thunder and lightning. Enter three Witches

First Witch	When shall we three meet again In thunder, lightning, or in rain?
Second Witch	When the hurlyburly's done, When the battle's lost and won.
Third Witch	That will be ere the set of sun.
First Witch	Where the place?
Second Witch	Upon the heath.
Third Witch	There to meet with Macbeth.
First Witch	I come, Graymalkin!
Second Witch	Paddock calls.
Third Witch	Anon.
All	Fair is foul, and foul is fair: Hover through the fog and filthy air.

Exeunt

The story ...

The three witches meet again. The second witch has been killing pigs. The first witch is angry with a sailor's wife who wouldn't share some chestnuts with her. The witch plans to take revenge on the sailor who is at sea in a ship called *The Tiger*.

What might the characters be thinking ...?

"Quite a good day's work causing trouble, but we could make that ship's captain suffer!"

Useful words ...

thou/thee you (**thou art** you are)

swine pigs

quoth said

aroint go away

rump fed ronyon rude name for a woman

Aleppo a town in Syria

thither to there

Macbeth Act I, Scene III

A heath near Forres.
Thunder. Enter the three Witches

First Witch	Where hast thou been, sister?
Second Witch	Killing swine.
Third Witch	Sister, where thou?
First Witch	A sailor's wife had chestnuts in her lap,
	And munch'd, and munch'd, and munch'd:
	'Give me,' quoth I:
	'Aroint thee, witch!' the rump-fed ronyon cries.
	Her husband's to Aleppo gone, master o' the Tiger:
	But in a sieve I'll thither sail,
	And, like a rat without a tail,
	I'll do, I'll do, and I'll do.
Second Witch	I'll give thee a wind.
First Witch	Thou'rt kind.
Third Witch	And I another.

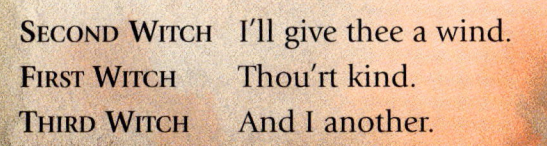

The story ...

The first witch decides on a curse to put on the sailor. The witches know that Macbeth is just about to appear.

What might the characters be thinking ...?

"We've got control of all the winds between us, so I can make that sailor's life on the sailing ship a real misery! I'll make sure he doesn't get any sleep for weeks and weeks. Even if the ship isn't wrecked I can still make sure it's in some terrible storms! I do like a good shipwreck though!"

Useful words ...

shipman's card sailor's compass

penthouse lid eyelids

seven-nights a week

dwindle, peak and pine be worn away

bark ship

tempest-tost thrown about by storms

Macbeth Act I, Scene III

FIRST WITCH   I myself have all the other,
And the very ports they blow,
All the quarters that they know
I' the shipman's card.
I will drain him dry as hay:
Sleep shall neither night nor day
Hang upon his penthouse lid;
He shall live a man forbid:
Weary seven-nights nine times nine
Shall he dwindle, peak and pine:
Though his bark cannot be lost,
Yet it shall be tempest-tost.

Look what I have.

SECOND WITCH   Show me, show me.

FIRST WITCH   Here I have a pilot's thumb,
Wreck'd as homeward he did come.

Drum within

THIRD WITCH   A drum, a drum!
Macbeth doth come.

The story ...

Macbeth and his friend Banquo meet the three witches for the first time. They are shocked by the witches' strange appearances.

What might the characters be thinking ...?

"We'll work together to make this spell for Macbeth a powerful one!"

"This is a very strange day ... What on earth...! Can they speak?"

"Are these humans? Are they women? They look completely wild!"

Useful words ...

thrice three times

Forres a town in Scotland

chappy rough, chapped

forbid me to interpret make it impossible for me to think

Macbeth Act 1, Scene III

ALL The weird sisters, hand in hand,
Posters of the sea and land,
Thus do go about, about:
Thrice to thine, and thrice to mine,
And thrice again, to make up nine.
Peace! the charm's wound up.

Enter Macbeth and Banquo

MACBETH So foul and fair a day I have not seen.

BANQUO How far is't call'd to Forres? – What are these
So wither'd and so wild in their attire,
That look not like the inhabitants o' the earth,
And yet are on't? Live you? Or are you aught
That man may question? You seem to understand me,
By each at once her chappy finger laying
Upon her skinny lips: you should be women,
And yet your beards forbid me to interpret
That you are so.

MACBETH Speak, if you can: what are you?

The story .....

The witches greet Macbeth as Thane of Glamis (a title he already has), Thane of Cawdor (which he is not), and future King of Scotland. Macbeth does not speak at first and Banquo is surprised by his friend's shocked reaction to prophecies that seem good. Banquo asks for a prophecy for his own future.

What might the characters be thinking …?

"What! Can they read my mind? I must act normally or Banquo will think I'm acting suspiciously."

"Why does Macbeth seem so shocked and frightened? It's not bad news to hear you might be King! What are these creatures? I'd like to know what they think is going to happen to me – I think I'll ask them."

Useful words ...

hereafter after this

start jump with surprise

rapt withal completely lost in his own thoughts

seeds of time the future

Macbeth Act 1, Scene III

FIRST WITCH All hail, Macbeth! hail to thee, Thane of Glamis!
SECOND WITCH All hail, Macbeth, hail to thee, Thane of Cawdor!
THIRD WITCH All hail, Macbeth, thou shalt be King hereafter!
BANQUO Good sir, why do you start; and seem to fear
Things that do sound so fair? I' the name of truth,
Are ye fantastical, or that indeed
Which outwardly ye show? My noble partner
You greet with present grace and great prediction
Of noble having and of royal hope,
That he seems rapt withal: to me you speak not.
If you can look into the seeds of time,
And say which grain will grow and which will not,
Speak then to me, who neither beg nor fear
Your favours nor your hate.

The story ...

The witches make predictions for Banquo, including the prophecy that his family will become king. When Macbeth realises the witches are about to disappear, he calls for them to stay.

What might the characters be thinking ...?

"What does that mean? They're talking in riddles. Banquo's family on the throne! I thought I'm the one who's going to be King!"

"Lesser but greater? Not so happy but happier? Father of Kings but not a King myself? What can this mean?"

Useful words ...

get beget (an old word for be the father of)

Macbeth Act I, Scene III

First Witch	Hail!
Second Witch	Hail!
Third Witch	Hail!
First Witch	Lesser than Macbeth, and greater.
Second Witch	Not so happy, yet much happier.
Third Witch	Thou shalt get kings, though thou be none: So all hail, Macbeth and Banquo!
First Witch	Banquo and Macbeth, all hail!
Macbeth	Stay, you imperfect speakers, tell me more …

Witches vanish

The story ...

Banquo and Macbeth discuss what the witches have said. Two messengers arrive from the King to tell Macbeth how pleased the King is with the way Macbeth fought in the battles.

What might the characters be thinking ...?

"They seemed real but they just melted in to thin air! This is really exciting but I must act coolly with Banquo. What are Ross and Angus doing here? Well, I'm glad that the King has been hearing such good things about me."

"They disappeared like bubbles in the air! Have we eaten some poisonous drug that's making us see these strange sights? Macbeth seems very excited. What are Ross and Angus doing here? Yes, it's fair that the King should have heard such fine things about Macbeth – he fought like a lion."

"It's good to be bringing some good news. Macbeth is a great soldier."

"There's a strange atmosphere in this place."

Useful words ...

whither where (or where to)

corporal flesh and blood

would if only

takes the reason prisoner a root that makes you go mad

selfsame exactly the same

thy your

bear carry

Macbeth Act I, Scene III

BANQUO	The earth hath bubbles, as the water has,
	And these are of them. Whither are they vanish'd?
MACBETH	Into the air; and what seem'd corporal melted
	As breath into the wind. Would they had stay'd!
BANQUO	Were such things here as we do speak about?
	Or have we eaten on the insane root
	That takes the reason prisoner?
MACBETH	Your children shall be kings.
BANQUO	You shall be King.
MACBETH	And Thane of Cawdor too: went it not so?
BANQUO	To the selfsame tune and words. Who's here?

Enter Ross and Angus

ROSS	The King hath happily received, Macbeth,
	The news of thy success …
	… As thick as hail
	Came post with post; and every one did bear
	Thy praises in his kingdom's great defence,
	And pour'd them down before him.

The story ...

Ross and Angus tell Macbeth that the King has decided to give him the title Thane of Cawdor because the former Thane has been a traitor to his King and country.

What might the characters be thinking ...?

"Thane of Cawdor! But Cawdor isn't dead! So ... two out of three prophecies have already come true – only one more to go ..."

"I can't believe this is happening! There's something evil about all of this."

"What is Banquo talking about? Why do they both look so shocked? The King was bound to honour Macbeth after the way he fought today."

"Cawdor deserves to die – the traitor. Macbeth will be a more honourable man."

Useful words ...

earnest sign

bade told

thine yours

treasons capital crimes against the King and country, serious enough to carry the death penalty

Macbeth Act I, Scene III

ANGUS	We are sent
	To give thee from our royal master thanks …
ROSS	And, for an **earnest** of a greater honour,
	He **bade** me, from him, call thee Thane of Cawdor:
	In which addition, hail, most worthy Thane!
	For it is **thine**.
BANQUO	What, can the devil speak true?
MACBETH	The Thane of Cawdor lives: why do you dress me
	In borrow'd robes?
ANGUS	Who was the Thane lives yet;
	But under heavy judgment bears that life
	Which he deserves to lose …
	… **treasons capital**, confess'd and proved,
	Have overthrown him.
MACBETH	*(Aside)* Glamis, and Thane of Cawdor!
	The greatest is behind.

The story ....

Time has passed and Macbeth has become an evil man. Confiding only in his wife, Lady Macbeth, he decided to murder the King who had honoured him in Act I. He murdered the King with a dagger while he was asleep and a guest at Macbeth's castle. Macbeth then became King of Scotland, as the witches had prophesied.

The King's sons, the rightful heirs to the throne, have fled to England where they are gathering an army to fight against Macbeth. Macduff, a powerful man and a soldier, becomes suspicious of Macbeth and leaves to join the army against Macbeth.

Macbeth has become obsessed with the witches' predictions and wants to stop Banquo's relatives becoming kings. Even though Banquo is his friend, Macbeth arranges to have him and his son murdered while they are out riding. The murderers kill Banquo but his son manages to escape, so in Macbeth's mind the witches' predictions for Banquo's family can still come true.

Both Macbeth and Lady Macbeth are becoming more and more troubled by the evil they have done. At a large public feast, Macbeth believes he can see the ghost of Banquo. No one else can see the ghost. Macbeth's behaviour is becoming suspicious and he has few friends in the court. He decides to go to find the witches again, in the hope that they will set his mind at rest. At the beginning of Act IV we see the witches making a magic potion in their cauldron.

Useful words ...

brinded striped

hedge-pig hedgehog

cauldron large pot

entrails guts

swelter'd venom poison sweated out

What might the characters be thinking ...?
"Let's make something really nasty before Macbeth arrives ..."

Macbeth Act IV, Scene 1

A cavern. In the middle, a boiling cauldron.
Thunder. Enter the three Witches

First Witch	Thrice the brinded cat hath mew'd.
Second Witch	Thrice and once the hedge-pig whined.
Third Witch	Harpier cries; 'Tis time, 'tis time.
First Witch	Round about the cauldron go;
	In the poison'd entrails throw.
	Toad, that under cold stone
	Days and nights has thirty-one
	Swelter'd venom sleeping got,
	Boil thou first i' the charmed pot.
All	Double, double toil and trouble;
	Fire burn, and cauldron bubble.

The story ...

The witches continue to boil up their magic potion.

What might the characters be thinking ...?

"Let's put in some really good ingredients ..."

Useful words ...

fillet strip of meat

fenny from the fens or marshland

maw mouth

ravin'd full (after eating its prey)

hemlock poisonous plant

gruel thin soup

slab slimy

chaudron guts

Macbeth Act IV, Scene 1

SECOND WITCH	Fillet of a fenny snake,
	In the cauldron boil and bake;
	Eye of newt and toe of frog,
	Wool of bat and tongue of dog,
	Adder's fork and blind-worm's sting,
	Lizard's leg and owlet's wing,
	For a charm of powerful trouble,
	Like a hell-broth boil and bubble.
ALL	Double, double toil and trouble;
	Fire burn and cauldron bubble.
THIRD WITCH	Scale of dragon, tooth of wolf,
	Witches' mummy, maw and gulf
	Of the ravin'd salt-sea shark,
	Root of hemlock digg'd i' the dark …
	… Finger of birth-strangled babe …
	Make the gruel thick and slab:
	Add thereto a tiger's chaudron,
	For the ingredients of our cauldron.
ALL	Double, double toil and trouble;
	Fire burn and cauldron bubble.
SECOND WITCH	Cool it with a baboon's blood,
	Then the charm is firm and good.

The story ...

Hecate, the witches' mistress, approves of the charm they have been making in their cauldron. Macbeth arrives.

What might the characters be thinking ...?

"Good! This will work well."

"They're here! But what are they doing?"

Useful words ...

commend praise

hags witches

Macbeth Act IV, Scene I

Enter Hecate (to the other three Witches)

HECATE O well done! I commend your pains;
And every one shall share i' the gains;
And now about the cauldron sing,
Like elves and fairies in a ring,
Enchanting all that you put in.

MUSIC AND Black spirits and white, red spirits and gray;
A SONG Mingle, mingle, mingle, you that mingle may.

Exit Hecate

SECOND WITCH By the pricking of my thumbs,
Something wicked this way comes.
Open, locks, whoever knocks!

Enter Macbeth

MACBETH How now, you secret, black, and midnight hags!
What is't you do?

ALL A deed without a name.

The story ...

Macbeth makes a desperate plea to the witches to answer the questions he wants to ask them. The witches invite him to hear the answers from their own masters.

What might the characters be thinking ...?

"They *must* answer my questions. I'll beg them to if necessary."

"He doesn't know what he's in for! Let's call up the masters!"

Useful words ...

conjure call upon

profess believe

yesty foaming

germens seeds

Macbeth Act IV, Scene 1

MACBETH	I conjure you, by that which you profess,
	Howe'er you come to know it, answer me:
	Though you untie the winds and let them fight
	Against the churches; though the yesty waves
	Confound and swallow navigation up;
	Though bladed corn be lodged and trees blown down;
	Though castles topple on their warders' heads;
	Though palaces and pyramids do slope
	Their heads to their foundations; though the treasure
	Of nature's germens tumble all together,
	Even till destruction sicken; answer me
	To what I ask you.
FIRST WITCH	Speak.
SECOND WITCH	Demand.
THIRD WITCH	We'll answer.
FIRST WITCH	Say, if thou'dst rather hear it from our mouths,
	Or from our masters?
MACBETH	Call 'em; let me see 'em.

The story ...

The witches conjure up the First Apparition, a head wearing armour, who warns Macbeth to beware of Macduff.

What might the characters be thinking ...?

"It'll begin with something he'll find easy to believe ..."

"Yes, Macduff! Just as I feared. Now I need to find out more ... but he's gone!"

Useful words ...

farrow piglets

gibbet gallows (used to hang people)

deftly quickly

apparition ghost

harp'd guessed

potent powerful

Macbeth Act IV, Scene 1

FIRST WITCH Pour in sow's blood, that hath eaten
Her nine farrow; grease that's sweaten
From the murderer's gibbet throw
Into the flame.

ALL Come, high or low;
Thyself and office deftly show!

Thunder. First Apparition: an Armed Head

MACBETH Tell me, thou unknown power –

FIRST WITCH He knows thy thought:
Hear his speech, but say thou nought.

FIRST APPARITION Macbeth! Macbeth! Macbeth! beware Macduff;
Beware the Thane of Fife. Dismiss me. Enough.

Descends

MACBETH Whate'er thou art, for thy good caution, thanks;
Thou hast harp'd my fear aright: but one word more –

FIRST WITCH He will not be commanded: here's another,
More potent than the first.

The story …

The Second Apparition, a bloody child, appears and tells Macbeth he cannot be harmed by a man born of a woman. The Third and most powerful Apparition appears: a child wearing a crown and holding a tree.

What might the characters be thinking …?

"This is an awful sight! 'None of woman born.' Then Macduff can't hurt me – I don't need to be afraid of him … But that seems to contradict what the First Apparition said …"

Useful words …

resolute determined

make assurance double sure make doubly sure

bond promise

Macbeth Act IV, Scene 1

Thunder. Second Apparition: A Bloody Child

Second Apparition	Macbeth! Macbeth! Macbeth!
Macbeth	Had I three ears, I'd hear thee.
Second Apparition	Be bloody, bold, and resolute; laugh to scorn The power of man, for none of woman born Shall harm Macbeth.

Descends

Macbeth	Then live, Macduff: what need I fear of thee? But yet I'll make assurance double sure, And take a bond of fate thou shalt not live; That I may tell pale-hearted fear it lies, And sleep in spite of thunder.

Thunder. Third Apparition: a Child crowned, with a tree in his hand

	What is this That rises like the issue of a king, And wears upon his baby-brow the round And top of sovereignty?
All	Listen, but speak not to't.

The story ...

The Third Apparition tells Macbeth that he won't be beaten until Birnam Wood moves to Dunsinane Hill. Macbeth believes this could never happen and that he will be safe. The spirits start to disappear, but Macbeth is desperate to hear that Banquo's descendants will not become kings. He demands that the spirits stay. The witches prepare to show him something that he will not like ...

What might the characters be thinking ...?

" Birnam Wood to Dunsinane! Impossible! Then I am safe. But I must know about Banquo's descendants ... Curse them! They must tell me!"

"He will not like this ... what a pleasant night's work!"

Useful words ...

lion-mettled with the courage of a lion

chafes ... frets irritates

conspirers people who make plots

vanquish'd beaten

bodements predictions

live the lease of nature live out his natural lifespan

pay his breath to time and mortal custom die naturally

issue children, descendants

Macbeth Act IV, Scene 1

THIRD APPARITION Be lion-mettled, proud; and take no care
Who chafes, who frets, or where conspirers are:
Macbeth shall never vanquish'd be until
Great Birnam Wood to high Dunsinane Hill
Shall come against him.

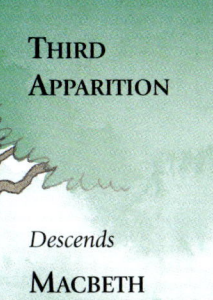

Descends

MACBETH That will never be
Who can impress the forest, bid the tree
Unfix his earth-bound root? Sweet bodements! good!
Rebellion's head, rise never till the wood
Of Birnam rise, and our high-placed Macbeth
Shall live the lease of nature, pay his breath
To time and mortal custom. Yet my heart
Throbs to know one thing: tell me, if your art
Can tell so much: shall Banquo's issue ever
Reign in this kingdom?

ALL Seek to know no more.

MACBETH I will be satisfied: deny me this,
And an eternal curse fall on you! Let me know.
Why sinks that cauldron? and what noise is this?

FIRST WITCH Show!

SECOND WITCH Show!

THIRD WITCH Show!

ALL Show his eyes, and grieve his heart;
Come like shadows, so depart!

The end of the story

Lady Macbeth dies a miserable death, wracked with guilt and unable to find peace. Macbeth prepares for the battle against the army from England at Dunsinane Hill. He seems to believe still in the witches' prophecies, but is badly shaken by the fact that the soldiers have stripped branches from the trees in Birnam Wood to use as camouflage. Birnam Wood has, in a sense, come to Dunsinane.

Nevertheless, Macbeth fights bravely, and kills many enemy soldiers. Finally he comes up against Macduff. He taunts Macduff, saying that no one born of woman can kill him. Macduff reveals that he was born by a Caesarean operation, which means that he was taken from his mother's womb rather than being born in the usual way. The witches' predictions have been both true and false. Macbeth realises that he has been deceived. Macduff kills Macbeth. The true heirs to the throne of Scotland can now reign – and Banquo's descendants can become kings.